CONTENTS

WHO IS ANITA RODDICK?

Anita Roddick created the Body Shop. She is famous, outspoken and a millionaire many times over. In 21 years she has built up the Body Shop from one shop in Brighton to an international business employing 3900 people in 47 countries.

Anita Roddick is more than a business person. Since she began the Body Shop she has turned the world of **cosmetics** upside down. She has changed the way cosmetics are sold, **marketed** and tested.

Anita Roddick
(centre left),
her husband
Gordon,
and their
daughters.

HEINEMANN
Profiles

Anita

Roddick

First published in Great Britain by
Heinemann Library
Halley Court, Jordan Hill,
Oxford OX2 8EJ
a division of Reed Educational and
Professional Publishing Ltd.
Heinemann is a registered trademark of
Reed Educational & Professional
Publishing Limited.

OXFORD MELBOURNE
AUCKLAND KUALA LUMPUR
SINGAPORE IBADAN NAIROBI
KAMPALA JOHANNESBURG
GABORONE PORTSMOUTH NH
CHICAGO

Designed by Visual Image, Taunton.
Printed in Hong Kong / China

Details of written sources:
Anita Roddick, *Body and Soul*,
HarperCollins, 1993

03 02 01 00 99
10 9 8 7 6 5 4 3 2 1

ISBN 0 431 08621 4

This title is also available in a hardback
library edition (ISBN 0 431 08620 6)

**British Library Cataloguing in
Publication Data**

Rob Alcraft
  Anita Roddick. – (Heinemann
  Profiles)
  1. Roddick, Anita – Juvenile literature
  2. Businesswoman – Great Britain –
  Biography – Juvenile literature
  3. Cosmetics industry – Great Britain –
  Juvenile literature
  338.4'7'66855'092

ISBN 0431086214

Acknowledgements
The Publishers would like to thank the
following for permission to reproduce
photographs: The Body Shop pp4, 7, 8,
12, 15, 16, 17, 18, 23 (bottom), 25, 31, 32,
34, 36, 39, 42 (both), 43, 45, 46, 48, 49
(all), 51, 52, 53; J Allan Cash Ltd p19;
Environmental Images p23 (top); Chris
Honeywell p39; Greenpeace/Morgan
p29; Oxford Scientific Films, M and P
Fogden p35, B Lehnhausen p30;
PowerStock Photo Library p27.

Cover photograph reproduced with
permission of Rex Features

Every effort has been made to contact
copyright holders of any material
reproduced in this book. Any omissions
will be rectified in subsequent printings if
notice is given to the Publisher.

Any words appearing in the text in bold,
like this, are explained in the Glossary.

HEINEMANN
Profiles

Anita

R

k

First published in Great Britain by
Heinemann Library
Halley Court, Jordan Hill,
Oxford OX2 8EJ
a division of Reed Educational and
Professional Publishing Ltd.
Heinemann is a registered trademark of
Reed Educational & Professional
Publishing Limited.

OXFORD MELBOURNE
AUCKLAND KUALA LUMPUR
SINGAPORE IBADAN NAIROBI
KAMPALA JOHANNESBURG
GABORONE PORTSMOUTH NH
CHICAGO

Designed by Visual Image, Taunton.
Printed in Hong Kong / China

Details of written sources:
Anita Roddick, *Body and Soul*,
HarperCollins, 1993

03 02 01 00 99
10 9 8 7 6 5 4 3 2 1

ISBN 0 431 08621 4

This title is also available in a hardback
library edition (ISBN 0 431 08620 6)

**British Library Cataloguing in
Publication Data**

Rob Alcraft
  Anita Roddick. – (Heinemann
  Profiles)
  1. Roddick, Anita – Juvenile literature
  2. Businesswoman – Great Britain –
  Biography – Juvenile literature
  3. Cosmetics industry – Great Britain –
  Juvenile literature
  338.4'7'66855'092

ISBN 0431086214

Acknowledgements
The Publishers would like to thank the
following for permission to reproduce
photographs: The Body Shop pp4, 7, 8,
12, 15, 16, 17, 18, 23 (bottom), 25, 31, 32,
34, 36, 39, 42 (both), 43, 45, 46, 48, 49
(all), 51, 52, 53; J Allan Cash Ltd p19;
Environmental Images p23 (top); Chris
Honeywell p39; Greenpeace/Morgan
p29; Oxford Scientific Films, M and P
Fogden p35, B Lehnhausen p30;
PowerStock Photo Library p27.

Cover photograph reproduced with
permission of Rex Features

Every effort has been made to contact
copyright holders of any material
reproduced in this book. Any omissions
will be rectified in subsequent printings if
notice is given to the Publisher.

Any words appearing in the text in bold,
like this, are explained in the Glossary.

The Body Shop

- over 1500 shops worldwide
- employs 3900 people
- 87.3 million customers a year

Anita is a campaigner, too. She has mixed shopping with conscience. From the beginning she refused to test her products on animals. She argues that it is wrong that thousands of animals should suffer in cosmetics experiments. 'Business can have a kinder face,' says Anita. She has campaigned to save the whale and rainforests. More recently she put the name of the Body Shop – with its presence in every high street – behind Comic Relief, and a **campaign** for **human rights** in Nigeria.

Everyone who meets Anita is struck by her energy and passion. She is always restless and looking for new excitement. Anita travels the world in search of new causes to support, and new products for her shops. Many people have tried to copy her success. 'If only,' she says 'they copied our principles, and not just our products.'

'I do not waste time lying in bed if I am not tired. I was born with energy. To me sleep is a kind of dying, and the moment I wake I must be up and doing something.'

Anita Roddick,
Sunday Telegraph, 3 February 1985

Growing up 'Different'

Anita was born in 1942 in Littlehampton, a small seaside town on the south coast of Britain. It was full of holiday-makers in the summer, quiet and wet in the winter.

Anita's mother, Gilda, divorced her first husband. When Anita was eight, Gilda married again, to a man called Henry Perella. Anita loved Henry and called him 'Uncle'.

Henry and Gilda ran an American-style café near the sea front. It was called the Clifton Café, and served up chips, cola and steaming mugs of coffee. It had a juke box and pinball machines and was *the* place to be in the early 1950s in Littlehampton.

'She [Gilda, Anita's mother] pushed all us kids (two sisters and one brother) on to the edge of bravery. The things she made us do! Every Saturday we had to do the shopping and she'd look at what we bought and say "Go back and tell the butcher there's too much fat." I mean, we'd only be about ten years old and we'd be there with all those big people saying, "Mummy doesn't like this." But it forced us to stand up for ourselves, because we were standing up for her.'

Anita Roddick, *Daily Mail*, 8 April 1996

A GIRL CALLED BUBBLES

After school Anita would help in the kitchen at the back of the café. She was dark-haired and cheeky, always talking and full of energy. At school they called her 'Bubbles'. At home she was always in trouble. She says now, 'I was a pain in the neck!'.

NOISE AND SHARING

Anita's family was very close. 'We were noisy,' says Anita, 'always screaming and shouting, we played music loudly, ate pasta and smelled of garlic.'

But although they were happy, there was never much money. The family all slept in the one room above the café. Her two sisters shared one bed, she shared with her mother, and her father slept behind a curtain at the other end of the room. The other rooms in the house were rented out to make money.

Anita in Littlehampton, the seaside town where she grew up.

Lessons from the 'Super Heroes'

Anita went to a Catholic convent school called
St Catherine's. Her teachers were nuns. They wore
robes and hats called wimples. Anita spent a lot of
her time trying to work out if, under their wimples,
they had shaved heads.

At school Anita learned how to make deals. Her
'Uncle' Henry, who had been living in America had
brought back a stack of colourful American action
comics. They were full of 'Super Heroes'
triumphing over villains. No-one at school had ever
seen anything like them and Anita found that she
had something everyone wanted. Suddenly boys
stopped calling her 'Bubbles' and were nice to her.
She could swap her comics for whole sets of
collectors' cards and movie albums.

Anita's mother, Gilda. She opened a night-club when Anita left home.

A secret beginning

Anita's life began with a secret. Her father was not who she thought he was.

Anita's mother, Gilda, came from a strict Italian family. Her marriage was arranged for her, so that when she fell in love with someone else, it was too late. Gilda married the man who had been chosen for her. But Gilda's arranged marriage was unhappy and she never forgot her first love, called Henry. One day, when Henry turned up on the doorstep, Gilda and he began a passionate affair. The children she had were Henry's, not her husband's. One of those children was Anita.

Anita was 19 before she found out. 'When Mummy told me I was **illegitimate** I nearly died with joy,' says Anita. 'I knew there would be something wild and creative in me.'

'Uncle' Henry, Anita's real father.

TRAGEDY

One day, when Anita was ten, she came home from school and found 'Uncle' Henry lying on the ground behind the Clifton Café, surrounded by a small crowd of people. He was dead. He had died from a disease called TB (tuberculosis).

Starting Out

Soon after Henry had died, Anita picked up a book about the **Holocaust** – the name given to the persecution and murder of Jewish people by the Nazis. She sat and read.

Book on the Holocaust

The awful pictures of **death camps** made her realize how much injustice there was in the world. She was sure she should do something to prevent this sort of unfairness, and try her best to help people. The book changed the way she thought. She went out and swapped her new school uniform with a girl whose own was old and tatty. She was going to be someone who thought about things and did something about them.

School

Anita moved to a new secondary school where the teachers made her more interested in school work. She discovered music, movies and an actor called

'I enjoy myself doing good …. When you do good in a community, the benefits get back to you. I can't believe that anyone would want to do the opposite.'

Anita Roddick, *Third Way*, January 1996

James Dean. She began to learn and read. Her mother used to say, 'You shouldn't read so much, you'll hurt your brain.'

Anita also loved to go out, have fun, and meet boys. It was the 1960s and Anita began to enjoy some of the new freedoms of the young generation. She went to the Top Hat Ballroom to go dancing, Butlin's for holidays, and carnivals and parties on the beach.

TEACHING

Ballroom dancing in 1960s Brighton.

By the time Anita was 18 she had passed her school exams and needed to earn a living. Eventually she decided to become a teacher. She began a course at the Newton Park Training College in Bath.

Anita has been travelling the world since she was aged 20. On this trip to Israel she worked at a farming community called a kibbutz.

WORK, TALK AND TRAVEL

'Listen, I'm the best and hardest worker you'll ever get. I love to work… .' It was 1963, Anita was 21, and talking herself into an administration job at the **United Nations** in Geneva, Switzerland. She could not type or do shorthand. In fact, she could not do any of the things they wanted. But luckily, she was able to talk her way into anything.

Anita had finished three years at teacher training college but had turned down her first teaching job. Teaching did not seem to offer enough excitement. Instead she took a job in Paris and from Paris she had come to Geneva and the United Nations.

The 'hippy trail'

It was the mid-1960s and far away, romantic places like Marrakech, Kathmandu and Tahiti were within the reach of ordinary people. The '**hippy trail**' had begun. Work was easy to find. You could earn money, leave your job, travel, and then pick up more work when you came home. It was a life Anita knew she would love. She left her job at the United Nations and boarded a boat for Tahiti, an island in the Pacific Ocean. From Tahiti she travelled to Australia, and then on to South Africa. While in South Africa she discovered jazz music.

The best jazz could be heard in black people's clubs. But at that time South Africa's **apartheid** system meant black and white people were not allowed to mix. Breaking the rules earned many black people long prison sentences. When Anita was spotted in a black people's club the police picked her up. They gave her 24 hours to leave the country. Anita left for home.

LOVE AND LITTLEHAMPTON

In 1964, on her first night at home in Littlehampton, Anita met Gordon Roddick. He was tall and quiet. Like Anita he had just returned from travelling the world. 'He said the minute he looked at me he knew he was doomed,' Anita joked later in a newspaper interview. Within four days Anita had moved into Gordon's little flat.

Anita had a job teaching in a junior school in Worthing. She left this job when she became pregnant. In August 1969 she gave birth to a baby girl, Justine. Anita and Gordon were happy, but now they had an extra mouth to feed. It was time to look around for ways of making money.

'It is not simply a case of complementary skills. Few professional managers could have handled Anita Roddick's manic brand of creativity. The secret is the personal chemistry. When they first met it was love at first sight. "We just knew" Anita told me of her first meeting with Gordon. "Our courtship lasted about four and a half minutes." '

Sunday Telegraph, 5 November 1995

MAKING MONEY

With the little savings they had, they opened a hotel in Littlehampton and then a restaurant. It was the Littlehampton restaurant that nearly lost them everything. For weeks they sat staring at empty tables. 'We thought we could impose our will on our customers and sell gourmet health food in an egg-and-chips town,' says Anita.

Anita with her
first daughter,
Justine.

'What saved us…was our willingness to recognize that we were wrong, and our ability to move swiftly on to our next idea.' For Anita it was an important lesson in business: when something is going wrong you have to change.

Anita and Gordon changed the menu to steak, burgers and chips. Soon they were spending most of their waking hours serving and cooking in the restaurant. Apart from the restaurant and hotel they now had a second daughter, Samantha, born in 1971. They had also become involved in local charities and causes. The restaurant became successful, but they were exhausted. After three years of running the hotel and restaurant, Gordon said, 'This is killing us. Let's pack it in.'

'She dreams and I try to make her dreams come true.'

Gordon Roddick

Setting Up Shop

At 34 Anita Roddick sat, scruffy and enthusiastic, with her two young daughters in front of her local bank manager. Excitedly shaking her thick mane of black hair, she explained her new idea. She would make and sell skin creams and shampoos. Unlike other **cosmetics**, there would be no fancy packaging and no testing on animals. Customers would be able to buy as little or as much as they wanted. The business would be called the Body Shop. All the bank manager had to do was lend her £4000. The bank manager said 'no'. He did not share Anita's wild enthusiasm.

Anita would not take 'no' for an answer and she went back again. This time she was smartly dressed and carried a **business plan** with pages of figures and projections – the sort of thing bank managers understand. Gordon went along, too. This time the bank manager took Anita's idea seriously. He said 'yes' to the loan.

The first Body Shop

At 9am on 27 March 1976 Anita opened her first shop. It was in a little cobbled street in Brighton and sold just 15 home-made products. There were five sizes of everything. The Body Shop

These rows of bottles are a familiar sight for any visitor to the Body Shop. The first bottles Anita used were cheap specimen bottles meant for hospitals.

A Body Shop poster advertising one of the earliest products – cocoa butter.

logo – now world famous – was designed by an art student who got £25 for the job.

Anita knew that the shop would have to make £300 a week to survive. It was a lot. But on that first day there were so many customers that at the end of the day she had £130 stuffed in her pockets. 'I was not just happy,' says Anita, 'I was euphoric.'

But it was going to be hard work. Gordon was leaving for a journey he had always dreamed of – a horseback ride through South America. For the next year Anita would be on her own.

Anita in the first Body Shop. She made her customers feel special, and they kept coming back for more.

A good idea

The Body Shop is different from other shops. It has a reputation for caring. The Body Shop cares about animals, about the environment and about people. If you shop there, the idea is that you can feel good about yourself.

The first Body Shop products had handwritten labels, there were pips in the elderflower cream and bits of cucumber in the cleansing cream. This was the unique appeal of the Body Shop; the products were natural with no added chemicals and no false claims, such as that they would make you look younger. They smelt nice and made you feel pampered.

HARD WORK

Running the shop alone was hard work. Anita had two small children, and very little money. The products in the shop were simple and as cheap as possible. The atmosphere was good and Anita made it all work by talking to customers and describing the products and what they did. Every morning, on the way to work, Anita would even lay a trail of strawberry essence along the pavement to the shop. People could *smell* how good the shop was.

LONG HOT SUMMER

The shop was a good idea but Anita was also lucky. The summer of 1976 was the hottest for years. Brighton was full of people on holiday. They bought skin creams and shampoo. Anita easily made the target of £300 a week. The story of the Body Shop had begun.

Brighton seafront in 1976. With hot weather and plenty of visitors, it was the perfect place for the Body Shop to succeed.

The grim neighbours

Anita is now very proud that the Body Shop has never spent a lot of money on **advertising**. But this began as an accident. Just as the shop was about to open, a letter from a firm of solicitors dropped through the door. Two undertakers were objecting to the name 'Body Shop'. They said it was bad taste, and bad for their business. They would take Anita to court unless she changed it.

Anita decided to call the local paper. She spun an emotional story of two grim undertakers who were trying to close down a shop run by a young mother who just wanted to sell shampoo. The paper printed the story, and Anita heard nothing more from her neighbours. She also got a lot of free **publicity**. This was the way to advertise – tell a good story and let someone else pay to publish it.

Sun and money

Anita Roddick – now director of an international company – cheerfully admits she knew nothing about business when she started. She has never been to business school or studied books about running a business.

As the long hot summer of 1976 blistered on, the little Body Shop did better and better. Before the summer was over Anita decided she wanted another shop and another challenge. Even the chore of filling her sample bottles from huge five-gallon containers did not put her off. She made all the products herself, sometimes mixing them in the bath!

'The original Body Shop was a series of brilliant accidents,' says Anita. 'It had a great smell, it had a funky name. It was positioned between two funeral parlours – that always caused controversy.'

ANOTHER SHOP

Anita looked around for another suitable place for a Body Shop, and decided on Chichester. It had plenty of shoppers, many of them young women who cared about how they looked but were tired of what traditional **cosmetics** companies were offering.

The first shop had not made enough **profit** to pay for the second. So she had to find another £4000. She had no luck with the banks but looked around for someone who had the money to lend. Eventually she found a local garage owner who said he would lend her the £4000 for a half–share of the Body Shop.

The second Body Shop, in Chichester. Anita wanted the building to stand out. With paint and imagination, it did.

THE·BODY·SHOP·

Weeks later, in South America, Gordon received a letter from Anita. She told him that she had agreed to the deal. Gordon wrote back asking her not to do it, but it was too late. Anita got her second shop, and the garage owner's share is now worth over £100,000,000.

SURVIVING

'You survive for the first year with little breakthroughs,' says Anita. 'I can remember, for example, the first week the Brighton shop took over £500, and then the first week that both shops together took £1000.'

There were still weeks in that first year when Anita took less than £150 – which was not enough to pay the bills. Anita knew little about **accounting** and had no interest in it. If a bill arrived she would simply keep the shop open until she made enough money to pay it.

GORDON COMES HOME

When Gordon came home he was impressed with what Anita had started. Soon he was helping out, doing the things he was good at and Anita hated. He did the accounts and paid the wages and, to Anita's delight, he took over the bottling.

In September 1977 friends of Anita and Gordon said how much they would like to open another Body

Many thousands of animals are used in laboratory experiments every year. Some are used to test medicines. Some are used just to test cosmetics. The Body Shop has never tested its products on animals.

Against Animal Testing

Anita has always been against testing **cosmetics** on animals. She believes tests on animals are cruel and pointless. Any Body Shop tests use human volunteers.

Shop in Hove. Then more friends opened another Body Shop in Bognor Regis. More and more Body Shop products were made and sold. They had to take on a herbalist, called Mark Constantine, to help make the vast quantities of skin creams and shampoos that were needed to fill the shelves.

MORE SHOPS

It was Gordon's idea not to open any more shops themselves, but to let other people find the money needed. These people could set up the shops and sell Body Shop products. They would get some of the **profit** and Anita and Gordon would get the rest without having to borrow from a bank. It was an arrangement called 'franchising'. The Body Shop began to expand.

'MS MEGA-MOUTH'

The Body Shop had come a long way since its birth in Brighton. In 1979 new Body Shops opened in Greece and Sweden. By 1982 – just six years after the opening of the first shop – a new shop was opening every two weeks.

The Body Shop began to make headlines in the newspapers and other media. *Cosmopolitan*, a glossy women's magazine, ran a story about the new shop in Covent Garden, London. Soon Anita was being invited on to daytime TV for interviews. She showed viewers how to make skin creams with avocados – and so spread the Body Shop name nationwide.

'I always enjoyed being interviewed, talking about the company and putting forward our ideas: it helps, I suppose that I have the reputation of being Ms Mega-Mouth.'

Anita Roddick

Normal people don't look like models, says this Body Shop poster. We all look different and we should be pleased about it.

Anita hates the **cosmetics** and 'beauty' industry. In one interview she said, 'The **marketing** is done by men, and they tend to ask each other the question "what are women frightened of this year?". If they come up with the answer "thick thighs", they produce something which claims to help. I think the beauty industry is old fashioned. We (the Body Shop) want to be involved in health care, skin care and environmental care, rather than beauty.'

London Evening Standard, 13 March 1985

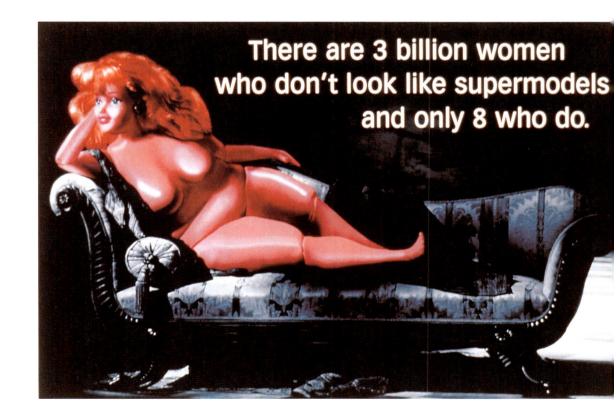

There are 3 billion women who don't look like supermodels and only 8 who do.

ANITA BECOMES A MILLIONAIRE

In 1984 the Body Shop was a worldwide business. Anita liked to say that every 0.7 seconds someone, somewhere, was buying a Body Shop product.

To keep the business growing Anita and Gordon needed yet more money. With more money they could invest and keep the Body Shop ahead of the competition. Anita and Gordon decided that the next important step was to 'go public'. This meant dividing the company into 'shares' which they could sell to the public. This would raise money to invest in the Body Shop. The people who bought shares – called shareholders – would receive part of each year's **profits** in return for their investment.

As the day of the sale approached, Anita attended more and more meetings with businessmen. There were many discussions, and many decisions to make.

STORMING THE STOCK MARKET

It was April 1984 in the **Stock Market** and the day for 'going public' had arrived. Everyone thought the Body Shop was doing so well that the starting price of 95p a share was cheap. They kept buying the shares, and the price rose all day. When trading was over each share was worth £1.65.

The Stock Market in London. It works like any other market, except that instead of fruit and vegetables, traders buy and sell company shares.

Anita and Gordon kept some shares which they did not sell. In this way they still owned the Body Shop and it was still theirs to control. Once added together their shares were now worth £1.5 million. Anita, only eight years after opening her first shop, was a millionaire.

'I can remember standing there behind the scenes. At nine o'clock a huge clock went dong and trading began. Four or five people began trading Body Shop shares immediately and we watched as the price went up from 95p, to £1, to £1.05, to £1.10. I have to admit the whole thing was thrilling. People were shouting and cheering... .'

Anita Roddick

Skin Care and Planet Care

In 1985 the Body Shop did something extraordinary. It launched an environmental **campaign**. No other chain of high street shops had ever attempted it. Anita did not think it was extraordinary: she said 'I have never been able to separate Body Shop values from my own personal values.'

Anita and Gordon had watched their business grow and succeed. They had taken the high street – and the **Stock Market** – by storm. They were millionaires and had shops all over the world. But they believed there were even more important things to do in life.

Making waves

Anita's first move was to work with Greenpeace. Greenpeace is an organization that campaigns against damage to the environment and to animals. The Body Shop paid for their posters to appear on billboards. The posters read 'Thank God someone's making waves', and showed a Greenpeace boat battling through the waves. The posters also showed people that they could join Greenpeace at their local Body Shop.

The Greenpeace flagship, Rainbow Warrior.

Anita learned that the **cosmetics** industry was using the oil from sperm whales in many products. The whales were being hunted to extinction for nothing more than vanity. The Body Shop had proved already that there were alternatives to using animal oils. They used jojoba oil, first used by Native Americans (on their hair and bodies), in skin creams and shampoos. And jojoba oil comes from plants, not animals.

Some types of whale have nearly disappeared because so many have been hunted and killed. The Body Shop helped launch an early campaign to protect whales.

'Save the Whale'

Anita's next **campaign** against whaling went one step further than the campaign the year before. It used Anita's own shops as billboards. It seemed simple and practical. They had two million customers passing through their shops everyday. They had another ten million walking past the windows. It was an excellent opportunity to inform people, not just about Body Shop products, but about things that mattered.

Anita was helping to prove that business could be **ethical**, and that it did have responsibilities beyond getting people to buy shampoo – however good – and then walk out the door. The Body Shop as a campaigning force had been born.

Anita is often travelling, meeting people and learning about how they live. Along the way she has discovered many new products for the Body Shop.

ACTIONS AND WORDS

The campaigns had made something else clear to Anita. Each campaign got the attention of the media. It brought more customers into the Body Shop. It also meant customers trusted the Body Shop not just to sell decent shampoo, but to do the right thing. 'They trust us to campaign,' says Anita, 'to continue to get the law changed on animal testing.'

By now, Anita was often being asked to speak and give talks. Other business people wanted to know about the success of the Body Shop and how it was trying to make business more caring. She also talked about her knowledge of peoples from around the world, gained while researching new Body Shop products. At one meeting in London at the end of 1987, just as she had finished speaking, a young man questioned her. Did she mean all she said about caring, or was it just a way of selling more Body Shop products?

Anita and staff from the Body Shop Soapworks' factory outside Glasgow.

A place called Easterhouse

The young man was a community worker from a place called Easterhouse outside Glasgow. Easterhouse was as poor as any of the places Anita had visited and talked about. There was no money, and no work. The housing was poor and run down. Young people had nowhere to go, and no hope of a job after school. If the Body Shop was eager to help whales, perhaps they could do something for people in Easterhouse.

Anita took up the challenge and went to visit Easterhouse. She found the people were keen to make their area better and she wanted to help them.

Soap is sense

Anita thought soap might be the answer. The Body Shop could build a new factory in Easterhouse for making soap. It would create jobs, and the Body Shop would run it so that 25 per cent of the **profits** went into community projects in the area.

Eight months later the Soapworks opened. Soon it employed a hundred people and was supplying soap to Body Shops all over the world. The Soapworks had shown that **fair trade,** as much as **campaigning**, could make a difference.

BRAZIL NUT OIL AND THE KAYAPO PEOPLE

By the 1980s **fair trade** was very much a part of Anita's ideas about business having a caring role. When Anita was invited to visit the Kayapo people, who lived in the rainforests of Brazil, she continued with the idea that trade could help.

As she sat in the large central hut of the Kayapo village, Anita talked with people about the Body Shop. She found that the Kayapo people were interested in harvesting and trading Brazil nut oil with the Body Shop. They could use the money from this trade to continue living in the rainforest. It meant having the money to bring the changes they wanted, without being exploited by outsiders.

Young Kayapo people welcome Anita in Brazil in 1988.

Today the Kayapo people harvest and process Brazil nut oil for the Body Shop. They also collect the colouring used by the Body Shop in its Mango Body Butter. For Anita this trade became the most interesting and fulfilling part of her work.

THE WORLD BURNS

The rainforest – a world resource that is under threat.

It was 1988, huge fires raged in the rainforests of Brazil as farmers and landowners were clearing the forest with fire. They wanted to raise cattle and have more land to farm. But once burnt, the forest would never return.

The rainforests are more than just trees. They help the world by supplying oxygen, which we need to breathe. And they hold many of the world's species of plants and insects.

In just one year 300,000 square kilometres, an area bigger than the UK, went up in smoke. The Body Shop joined the international outcry. Posters, leaflets and petitions appeared in every shop. The message was simple: 'Stop the Burning'.

The Body Shop collected thousands of letters addressed to the president of Brazil, asking him to stop destroying the rainforests. Anita and 150 Body Shop staff delivered them personally to the Brazilian Embassy in London. No-one there would take them and eventually the police were called. This made headlines around the world on television and in the newspapers – it was brilliant **publicity**.

A Body Shop poster. The Body Shop has always been good at publicity and advertising.

COMMUNITY TRADE PROGRAMME

In the 1990s the Body Shop set up its own Community Trade Programme. It is trading now with 20 communities in 13 countries. The trade makes a **profit**, but it also helps poorer communities to support themselves. 'It's about respect, friendship and trust,' says Anita.

'Trade not Aid'

Some companies look for people anywhere in the world that will work for low wages. Low wages mean that these people will always be poor and their lives will be difficult. When Anita travelled she looked for better ways to work with the poorer communities, so that they would benefit directly from the products the Body Shop sold. Anita wanted to make life better for people, not worse.

Anita called the new policy 'Trade not Aid'. Sometimes it was difficult but Anita didn't give up.

'Teddy'

One trade project that worked well was given the unlikely name of 'Teddy'. It is based in Tirumangalam in southern India. A factory there makes wooden massage rollers and cotton cosmetic bags. These are sold in Body Shops round the world.

The Teddy factory employs nearly 300 people. 'Workers are supplied with free uniforms, lunch, tea and health care for themselves and their families,' says Anita. 'Each time something is bought from Teddy Exports 20 per cent is added to the price. What happens to the money is exceptional – it funds the activities of the Teddy Trust, Teddy Primary School and Teddy Trust Clinic [all in Tirumangalam].' This is Anita's idea of trade that works to make people's lives better, and it makes a profit.

BODY TROUBLE

S even years had gone by since the **Stock Market** had launched the Body Shop's shares. In that time many other famous businesses had gone bust. But the Body Shop had survived and grown.

But during 11 months in 1993 the price of Body Shop shares – the test of how healthy people thought the business was – began to plummet. Shareholders were nervous. They were all trying to sell their shares at the same time. At one point the Body Shop lost more than half its value.

BODY SHOP UNDER ATTACK

In the same year an American magazine published a story attacking Anita and the Body Shop. It said her record on the environment and animal testing was not good. Rumours flew around the newspapers and magazines in the UK and America.

In two weeks many articles appeared in the press. 'Halo slips on the raspberry bubbles' and 'Red face time for green Roddicks' were just a couple of the headlines. One morning Anita picked up the *Guardian* newspaper and read a story that claimed the RSPCA (Royal Society for the Prevention of Cruelty to Animals) had told its supporters to boycott the Body Shop because Anita's Against Animal Testing policy was flawed.

> 'If you wear a bullseye on your back saying "I'm doing things differently," you're going to get shot at. We're too interesting a company not to take pot shots at.'
>
> Anita Roddick, *Third Way*, 1996

In the 1990s, the Body Shop has suffered serious setbacks. It survived, kept its good name and kept making profits.

Then Channel 4 Television ran a documentary on the Body Shop. The programme questioned the honesty of the Body Shop. Like the article in the *Guardian* the programme said the Body Shop could not claim to be against animal testing.

Anita and Gordon decided to **sue** and take the people who made the programme to court. They were determined to prove them wrong.

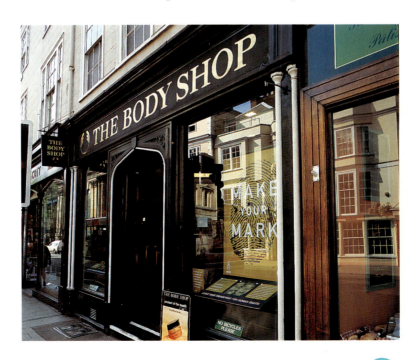

Body damage

Though the rumours and stories were untrue, they hurt the Body Shop and the share price continued to fall. Anita and Gordon launched a counter-attack, trying to restore their good name. 'The company does not pretend to be perfect or to have all the answers,' said their statement, and then it explained that Body Shop staff and customers were doing their best for the environment.

An inquiry was launched by one **ethical investment agency**. They said the Body Shop had been 'unfairly treated'. Many other supporters and experts joined in praising the efforts of Anita and the Body Shop. The RSPCA wrote to say, 'We acknowledge the contribution which the Body Shop has made, with others, in raising public awareness of the use of animals in **cosmetics** testing.'

Anita fights back

In 1993 the case against the Channel 4 programme came to court. Although Anita and Gordon won, it affected them deeply. 'My parents were completely broken during the court case,' says Justine, their eldest daughter. 'They completely lost their sparkle, and I got so upset for them.'

Anita and the Body Shop had fought off their critics. And now they said they would try even harder: they would do more trade directly with poor communities. Their record on the environment and good causes would be even better. The trial by media was over.

'I found myself,' wrote Anita, 'taking long cold looks at what we do and why we do it – and why it seems to make so many other people either nervous, vindictive or both.' Anita felt she was being attacked not for failing, but for trying. The Body Shop might get things wrong. It might not be perfect. But it would carry on trying.

Getting it right

Since 1994 the Body Shop has tested itself by setting up a special department that makes sure that the business reaches the right standards. The department looks at how well the company serves the environment, protects animals, and checks it treats people fairly. If the Body Shop fails its own test, it tries to put things right.

LIFE TODAY

Anita spends more and more of her time on personal missions. She wants to learn, listen, and, if she can, act. Sometimes it has nothing to do with selling products. Anita knows this. 'I'd rather promote **human rights**,' she says, 'than a bubble bath.'

VISITING THE FRONT LINE

In late 1996 Anita arrived at Heathrow Airport, outside London. She was travelling to Bosnia, a small country in southern Europe, with a group called Human Rights Watch. Much of the country had been destroyed by war and although the shooting had stopped there were still thousands of people who had lost everything.

A Romanian orphanage decorated by Body Shop volunteers. This is one of several projects that the Body Shop supports with money and time.

The Body Shop has worked with Amnesty to campaign for people's rights and freedom.

Human Rights Watch was trying to record what was happening, and get help to some of those who needed it. The Body Shop had been supporting them with small amounts of money and now Anita wanted to see if there was anything more she and the Body Shop could do.

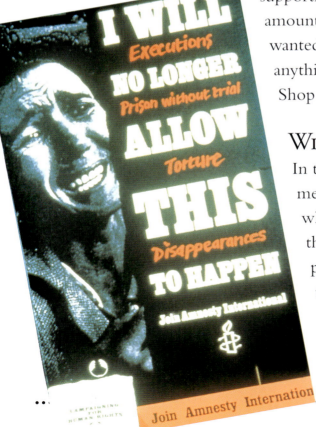

WITNESS

In the city of Sarajevo Anita met a group of six young men who were in hospital. All of them had lost limbs or been paralysed in the war. They told Anita they wanted to set up a printing house, learn new skills and rebuild their lives.

> 'Does it [**campaigning**] ever create a sale? The unfortunate thing is it doesn't. When people come in to sign a petition they don't then say, "Oh, by the way I want a moisture cream." '
>
> Anita Roddick

Once back in Britain, Anita got the Body Shop to increase the amount of money it gave to **Human Rights** Watch. She discussed ways in which the Body Shop could support people like the young men she had met.

> We are brilliant at publicizing issues. We have thousands of shops around the world, we can reach millions of people. When we worked with **Amnesty**, for example, we leveraged so many letters about the 30 prisoners of conscience we were campaigning for that 17 were released. That's brilliant!
>
> Anita Roddick

WHIRL OF ACTIVITY

Anita's life has become a whirl of travel, meetings, lectures and conferences. 'Money has given me immense freedom,' she says. It is a freedom she uses – always travelling, always wanting to experience new things. In April 1997, Anita spent a weekend with a man who is building and painting his own mountain. The 66-year-old lives outside Baltimore in the USA and his mountain is made of mud and water. It is a statement of his beliefs about life and God.

Business students are taught how to care for their customers at the New Business Academy in Bath.

Anita admires the bizarre. Committed people interest her – people like the man who is building his own mountain. She likes to be around people who do things, and who try to change things.

TALKING AND WRITING

Everywhere Anita goes she talks about the experiences and aims of the Body Shop. She has even begun a business school called the New Business Academy, in Bath. It is based on her vision of caring companies and concentrates not just on **profit** and loss but how business can make the world better, treating staff and the environment with care.

Anita has also written a regular newspaper column. It talks, tells stories, lectures, nags and exposes. One week it will be about her travels and the next about the latest campaign that has stirred her. The column is just like Anita's life – a mixture of all that interests her, injected with passion.

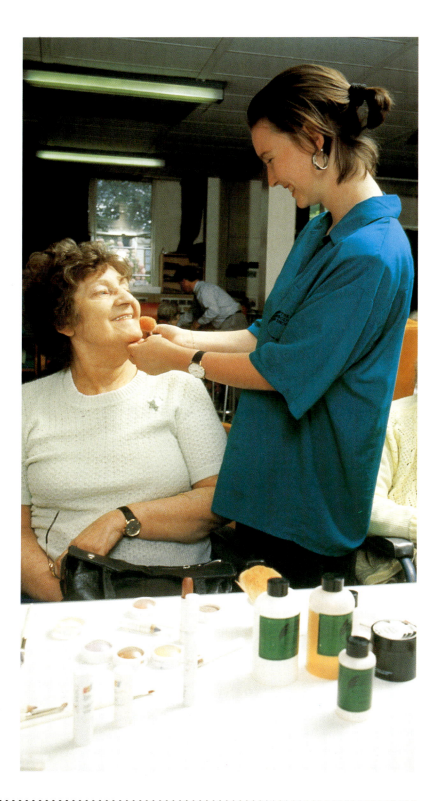

Staff at the Body Shop have the chance to take time off from work to help community projects in their area.

Buying back the Body Shop

Anita has often felt held back by the need to please shareholders. They are interested mainly in **profit** and do not share her passion for the bizarre. In 1995 she and Gordon tried to find a way to buy the Body Shop back from its shareholders. They wanted to be a private company again. But, for the moment, the Body Shop is worth more than Anita and Gordon can pay. They have control of the business but do not own it completely.

Littlehampton revisited

Littlehampton, where Anita was born, is still a quiet seaside resort. But on the road into town there are now giant Body Shop offices. They look a little like an eastern temple, with sloping roofs and green tiles. Life-size figures lounge on the grass. More of them swim in an ornamental pond. A billboard by the car park demands 'Flabby thighs, fat lips? Love your body'. Here the Body Shop is advertising not what it sells, but what it believes in.

There is even a guided tour of the factory. Visitors pay for the busy trail through the history of the Body Shop. Anita's first shop has been re-created, you can see the giant factory kitchen where they make the lotions and creams, and you can even follow those familiar Body Shop bottles on their journey along a huge conveyor belt.

Everything is here to see, except Anita. She is travelling or lecturing or **campaigning**. She has become one of the most talked about and recognized businesswomen in Britain. Like her company she is unorthodox and different. 'I admit I am driven,' says Anita, 'but I wouldn't change how I've done anything.'

'A lot of what I do is stimulate ideas. Gordon's job is to oversee the finances and keep my feet reasonably near the ground. I talk all day, goading on the staff, asking questions and keeping the company breathless and motivated. I pause for a mid-morning coffee and a sandwich for lunch, washed down with ice-cold water and camomile tea. If I'm hungry I steal Gordon's apple.'

Anita Roddick

The Body Shop
tries to make
people sit up
and notice its
advertising

Looking at Anita

'If I'd wanted to be quiet,' says Anita, 'I would have opened a library.' Everyone agrees; Anita is never quiet. She has energy and she speaks out whenever she thinks she can make a difference. She has **campaigned** about everything, from stopping tests on animals to getting housing for homeless people.

Friends and enemies

Because Anita is so outspoken she makes enemies. Many journalists are provoked by what they call her 'nagging'. They are keen to point out the times when she does not live up to her own standards. 'Critics snigger at her breathless denunciations of the wider **cosmetics** industry,' wrote a journalist from the *Sunday Telegraph* in 1997, 'when her shops are full of plastic-wrapped boxes, scented candles and other testaments to **throwaway consumerism**.'

Other people are suspicious of her reasons for campaigning. They say she promotes her business on the back of good causes. A journalist for the *Sunday Telegraph* wrote 'Anita has often been scornful of **advertising**, proudly saying that the Body Shop has no need of it, as she can generate all the **publicity** it needs. Yet last year we saw the "Queen of Green" chatting away on television about paying for visits to foreign tribes with her American Express card.'

Anita with a market woman selling cocoa butter. She says of the Body Shop 'I sometimes feel I'm in the wrong clothes. I shouldn't be anywhere near this company. It's so big now.'

Even some staff from the Body Shop feel Anita is too much. 'I began to hate the face of Anita Roddick telling me it was my duty to save the world,' said one member of staff who left, 'when all I wanted to do was go home and put my feet up. All that love and holding hands at staff meetings just got too much for me.'

But whether they like her ideas or not, most people agree that Anita believes what she says. '…she is definitely sincere, if a little naive,' says one journalist.

THE WOMAN PEOPLE WANT TO BE LIKE

Anita's sincerity and willingness to be a target also make her popular. In a 1996 survey she beat the model Naomi Campbell as the woman young girls most admired and wanted to be like. It was not because she was successful, but because she is willing to do the right thing, whatever the cost or the criticism.

Anita Roddick has won a string of awards. She has been named Communicator of the Year, Business Leader of the Year, and she has been awarded the OBE (Order of the British Empire). She is in demand as a speaker. People all over the world seek her views on how to combine business success with **ethics**.

Anita has won many awards for her work with the Body Shop.

'There is no doubting her achievement,' says one business person from the City. 'From nothing she has built a hugely successful – and important – company employing thousands of people and bringing great **profits** to her shareholders.'

So what if she's not perfect?

Many people are also impressed by the high standards Anita sets. 'As a high street store I think they [the Body Shop] are excellent,' says an organization called Beauty Without Cruelty. 'They were the original arbiter of not testing on animals, they are easily accessible to everyone and they genuinely try to be true to their high standards.'

The Body Shop tries to make its customers into friends, just as Anita did in her first shop in Brighton, over 20 years ago.

But perhaps only one opinion of Anita matters: the opinion of her customers who keep on coming back for more. She has inspired their loyalty in a way few other shops or business people could dream off. 'People slag her off because she's a successful business-woman and because she is passionate and outspoken,' said one customer buying camomile shampoo at the Body Shop. 'So what if she isn't perfect – at least she's trying which is more than most businessmen can say.'

It's your body and we love it

 THE BODY SHOP

Anita Roddick – Timeline

1942 Anita Perella born in Littlehampton, Sussex

1950 Anita's mother, Gilda, marries Henry Perella

1963 Anita begins to travel

1964 Anita meets Gordon Roddick

1969 Justine, first daughter born

1971 Anita marries Gordon Roddick in Reno, Nevada

Samantha, second daughter born

1976 First Body Shop opens in Brighton

1977 Gordon comes home from South America

1984 Body Shop goes public, and sell shares on the **Stock Market**

1985 Body Shop begins a **campaign** with Greenpeace, the first business to work with a charity

1993 Anita takes Channel 4 Television to court for false accusations of dishonesty. Anita wins

1994 Body Shop sets up Community Trade Programme

1995 Anita and Gordon think about buying Body Shop back from its shareholders

1996 Anita visits Bosnia. Travel and campaigning takes up much of her time.

GLOSSARY

accounting making a record of all the money spent and received by a company

advertising appears on television and in newspapers. It tries to make people buy things

Amnesty International an organization that tries to get innocent people freed from prison

apartheid a system used in South Africa to keep black and white people apart

business plan a report showing how a business might grow

campaign action by people who want to change laws, or make something happen

contradiction two opposite things which don't agree

cosmetics things like lipstick, shampoo and skin cream

death camps places where thousands of people are murdered

ethical investment company a company that puts money into products that do not harm people or the environment

ethics a set of beliefs about what is right and wrong

fair trade trade that tries to help poor communities

hippy trail a name for travel and adventure in the 1960s

Holocaust persecution of the Jews by the Nazis in the Second World War

human rights a set of things that everyone, wherever they live, has the right to

illegitimate someone whose mother and father were not married when they were born (an old-fashioned word that is not used very often as most people now think it doesn't matter)

marketing the way products are presented, what they are called, and how they are sold

profit the money left after a company has paid all its bills

publicity is making sure people have heard about you, and know what you do

Stock Market a place where shares in companies and businesses are bought and sold

sue taking someone to court because they have said bad things about you

throwaway consumerism buying things with lots of packaging that you don't need

United Nations a club, which most countries are members of so that they can discuss things that concern them all

INDEX